Dodge
The
Rain

K.C. Kemp

Printed in the United States of America
Cover art by Qzoh

ISBN-13:
978-09977343-0-0

ISBN-10:
0-9977343-0-2

DEDICATION

To my beautiful wife,
Thank you.
You are my inspiration.
My compass.
Without you none of this would have been
possible.
I would never have found myself.
I love you.

To My brother
Thank you
For showing me the meaning of true loyalty and
trust.
We are always side by side,
No matter the miles.

To my father
Thank you,
For your guidance and example
Of true strength,
No matter where
Life takes you.

To my mother
Thank you for your wisdom and love,
For your ability to find the light
In the darkest corner,
And fight for it.

To all who took the time to read this.
Thank you, this is for you.

CONTENTS

12.	CLICHÉ
13.	WILDFLOWER
14.	FIND IT ALL
15.	INTO THE AIR
16.	MOONSHINE
17.	RISE TO HONOR
18.	UNIVERSE
19.	FORGED OF IRON
20.	THE SHIPS
21.	SEEKERS
23.	EMPTY SKY
24.	THE KEY
25.	MOON & STARS
27.	A LITTLE MORE
28.	DEVIL'S HOPYARD
29.	RUN
31.	LOYAL
33.	CHARCOAL CLOUDS & OCHRE DUST
34.	GHOSTS
35.	HEAVY HANDED FOOLS
36.	SITTING WITH OWLS
37.	SOMEWHERE
38.	STORIES
40.	WAX WINGS
41.	THE NAVIGATOR
42.	IMPRESSIONS
43.	THE UNLOVED
44.	SILENCE
45.	HEAVY SOUL
47.	ALIVE
48.	HALF A LIFETIME

49. FRAGILE
50. DODGE THE RAIN
51. SCARS OF DIAMOND
52. BLOOM INTO ETERNITY
53. SPECTRUM
54. THE KARMAPA
56. STARFIRE
57. THUNDER-BEINGS
58. LOVE TOO HARD
59. MOVES THE SUN & STARS
60. SEE FOREVER
61. GUIDE YOU
62. CHANCE TO FEEL
64. HORIZON
65. DAWN
66. BLACKBIRD
68. TRUE STRENGTH
69. PAINT THE SKY
70. PHEONIX
72. WOLVES KNOW BETTER
73. DOG JOKES
74. STOCKHOLM SYNDROME
75. DREAMCATCHER
76. HANDS OF TIME
77. TIME
78. TODAY
79. SEIZE THE NIGHT
80. MEMORIES REMAIN
81. DRINK THE RAIN
82. DEFINE YOU
83. CHASING SHADOWS
84. MERMAID

85.	POET WITH A BLIND EYE
86.	RICOCHET
87.	FIGHT FOR HER
88.	CURSED BY HINDSIGHT
89.	AGE OF MIND
90.	FIREFLIES
91.	STALE WORDS
93.	CHILDREN OF EARTH
94.	SPARROW
96.	SEEDS OF STARDUST
97.	WHO WE ARE
98.	THE WILD ONE
99.	MIND OF A GIANT
100.	OPINIONS OF THE LOST
101.	SOMETHING MORE
102.	WITH A SMILE
103.	LIGHTHOUSE
104.	WHISKEY & AMARETTO
105.	LOST & FOUND
106.	SETTING SUN
107.	RIDE MOUNTAINS
108.	WILD
109.	PATCHWORK QUILT
110.	FOGGY NIGHT
111.	THE ANGELS
112.	REBUILT
113.	MATCHES
114.	MIRACLE
115.	STAR DREAMERS
116.	ST. FRANCIS
117.	MOTHER NATURE
118.	FIGHT

119. OUR SCARS
120. SOULLESS
121. LEAVE IT WITH ME
122. PRIDE
123. SOMETHING ROTTEN
124. THOUGHTS
125. CONSTELLATIONS
126. MASON
127. GALLERY
128. HEARTS OF GOLD
129. ATTACHMENTS
130. STRANGERS
131. ROULETTE & SIX-SHOOTERS
132. WHISKEY EYES
133. PARIS IN SEPTEMBER
134. IMMORTAL
135. SUNSTONE
136. IMPLODE
137. CLOSER TO GOD
138. COST OF LANDING
140. 4:30AM
141. PASSION
142. STOOD WITH YOU
143. WISE SOUL
144. ARMOR
145. AWARE
146. SECRETS
147. WITH YOU

Love a little harder in the rain;

Let it wash away who we think we are.

So we might find what we are made of.

Walking
Too slowly
Burning
Through
Daylight
Walking
Through
Day dreams.

Cliché

I listened
as she spoke
of how she had stood
alone
on the darkest night.

The way
the moon
would stay out of sight;
eclipsed;
hidden
under a blanket of
charcoal clouds.

I couldn't say much
looking into those
burnt umber eyes.

Ablaze
with the wisdom
of a hundred lives.

I offered an old cliché,
and she smiled.

Wildflower

She lost sleep.
Worried her dreams
may not remember her name.

She stays up all night
tossing and turning.
She shuts people out,
and sometimes,
that's a good thing.

She would listen to the birds.
They always had something
good to say.

It wasn't complicated,
and she didn't need
to make sense of it all.

They left
wildflowers
blooming in her heart,

that would remind her

of something more.

Find It All

I need to find it all.
All the chaos
All the tranquility
All the madness
All the serenity
All the fight
All the peace
I need to find all of you,
and all of me.

I need your dreams
to find me while I sleep.
But I find I do not want
to close my eyes,
and allow this moment
to slip through my cracks.

I need to find your darkness.
To feel it surround me so I can
dream in your scent,

and I need your light to wake the sky
so I can find it all again.

Into The Air

There is beauty in loneliness.
Salvation
in a night sky.

There is more
of you
in each whisper
of wind
than all of
that noise
out there.

Just drift
into the air,
and let it take you

into all the moments
that left us
breathless,
and hear yourself.

Be free.

Moonshine

I like these nights
standing alone.

You hear every sound
dogs bark on the street.

Moon shines down
staring through the centuries.

The smell of the night
always takes me
back
by your side.

Rise To Honor

Generations come and go.
Legends rise to fall,
to honor,
or from grace.
This is your time
to rise.

I have seen the sun
that burns
blindly
beneath your skin,

piercing through
the jagged edges
you so gracefully
smooth away.

The same edges
that cut
through all the bullshit,
and make knowing you
an honor.

Universe

She held galaxies
in her eyes,
and I'm not just saying that.

There were fucking stars
burning in her eyes.
Auroras shimmering
on the surface,
and deep black holes
that led to the center
of the universe.

A place that would cause
my simple mind to erupt
into a trillion birds.

Each finding its way
through a pinhole to the heavens,

then, falling back into human form
never to utter a single word.

For fear it was all my imagination.

Forged Of Iron

Those that sit
on horses high will follow
the one with the gold and silk.

If that one should fall
They will follow no more
and trample
over them just as quick.

The wounds worn
from the battles lost
will turn to scars
as hard as iron.

Whilst those that sit
on horses high, trot on,
and pass their judgment.

When the battle comes
They'll turn and run,

because they are not forged
of iron.

The Ships

Foundations
crumble with age.
We tend
not to maintain
the things
buried
within us.

Content to
settle
where we stand.

To watch the light
sink towards
that unspoken place
where dreamers meet with gods.

Lost in the wind
with the ships
that fell off
the face of the earth,
and found the stars.

Seekers

Seek the one
who finds peace
in the chaos
of a storm.

Stand with those
who shiver
in the cold
whilst others
seek the warmth.

Walk
with those
who can't stand
sitting still
watching the world
run wild.

Watch the one
who still looks
through the eyes
of a child.

We are
the dreamers

riding the mountains.

The unbroken spirits
drink
from life's fountain.

Empty Sky

Women capture starlight
with their eyes,
and cast it
on a man's shadow.

But this one,
she could take your soul,
and you wouldn't say a word.

In case
those eyes
should look
away,

and all you
would see
is an empty sky.

The Key

She is the key,

unlocks
a caged heart.
Runs with
a wild spirit
to catch the falling stars.

Strength
to hold
the world.

When Atlas trembles,

She will never
show
the burden.

Moon & Stars

I wonder
when looking at
the moon and stars,

Knowing
the same sky I see
could shine
on you.

Despite
the distance
between us,
and the way
time doesn't
always add up.

You could be
a day ahead of me
depending
on the hands
of a clock.

But if we look
up at that sky
at the same time,
and see

the moon & stars.

Just for a moment,
we have done
the impossible.

We are
together
through time
and space.

Just looking at the
same place.

A Little More

There is always more to learn,
always more to love.

Love will always find more.
More magic,
more pain,
Love will wish a little harder on a starry night,
and fall into the horizon with our eyes.
Love will feel a little more of the rain,
and dance alone when all else
has washed away,

The more I learned of her
the more I loved her,
and the minute you think
you love someone
you learn a little more.
More about them,
and more about yourself.
More than you could ever know
on your own.

We taught each other this,
and what it is
to love a little more.

Devil's Hopyard

Through trails
of embers and ash
in chaos.
A place they said
nothing
could last.

I carved our names
into that tree
in the devil's hopyard.

A love that has been to hell and back,
and made it through the fire.

That tree still stands
where I carved our names,
into heart shaped bark.

Walking with you
hand in hand
through
the devil's hopyard.

Run

There are those
that run
crooked roads

in search
of man-made gold.

All
that they
touch
turns to ash,
and burns.

But my son
we will carry on.
For you my son
we will run.
and run

until we run
them into
the ground.

In those places
where they
fear to go.

We will conquer
these places,
and call them
our own.

Loyal

I'd follow you
to the edge of the world
I proved it to you
that day.

When we walked together
lost,
and my faithful four legs
gave way.

I fell
panting and heaving,

I thought I failed you
that day.

My tired eyes
pleading
with you
not to stay.

But you put me around
your shoulders,

I knew we'd be ok.

You carried me
as the dark of night
began
to slowly
make its way.

But I knew we'd be ok.

For three
whole days
I couldn't move
I was resigned
to my fate.

But each night
your gentle hand
would feed me
and keep me safe.

So those
faithful four legs
of mine could rise
and stand again,

They may move
a little slower now
but I'd follow you
until the end.

Charcoal Clouds &
Ochre Dust

Surround me

With charcoal

Storm clouds

Drag me

Through

Ochre dust

I'll still

Lift you up

And always

Carry you

My love.

Ghosts

She said
she felt invisible.
like a ghost.

Floating
through walls all her life,
from one broken home
to another.

She picked
through the debris
as she floated
invisibly.

She built herself a tower
to see
beyond the walls,

and as she watched
the people walk by
she could see
through them all.

Heavy Handed Fools

Look in her eyes.

Listen to her thoughts.

Calm her nerves.

She does not
owe you her heart.

She keeps it;
locked away in pieces
broken
by heavy handed fools.

Be patient
only then can you unlock it,
and attempt
to put the pieces back.

Love is patient......
Love is enduring.......

Sitting with owls

Is it unwise to keep the hours of an owl in search of some wisdom?

Some enjoy watching the moon set.
I often do,

as I sit with the owls;

The early birds begin their morning chorus. They're much louder before the light, as if their melodies usher in the sun, or perhaps they are just fighting over the coveted worm, blindly squawking in the dark.

Pardon my cynical thoughts,
a mockingbird has begun his a cappella.
Ironic, as the song that ushers in the sun mocks my attempts to dream of you.

Well, I'll sleep in death; as they say; I just hope I dream of you.

Some enjoy watching the moon set.
I often do,
as I sit with the owls.

I want to take you to a place.

Somewhere we become lost in each other.
Somewhere time stands still.
Somewhere never to be found again,

Remember this moment......
This is our somewhere.

Stories

Watching people
walk by
all the stories
we will never know.

You feel them
filled with
the hope
the despair
the love
the pain.

It all
burns in us
with a violent wind.

Some kept in
old photographs
when it is all
said and done.

Found in a box of memories.
left for others
to piece together.

The stories
we could
never tell.

That made us

feel alive.

Wax wings

I held myself
too high
to fall
was inevitable,

Watching the world
pass me by
kissed the sun as I soar
through the sky.

When my waning
wings of wax,
began to melt
from my back.

The Navigator

Somehow, the navigator will find the way;
riding locomotives like a drifter.

Navigating the dark winding maze of caverns
that hold many a lost soul;
trapped, fallen,
from trains
of thought
that whistle by
searing through the silence
like a hot iron on supple skin.
Scarring locomotives that haunt
the dark winding, endless, crooked,
maze of caverns
littered with the remnants of men's will;
picked apart until unrecognizable
crushed under the weight of its own train of thought.

Somehow, the navigator will find the way;
riding locomotives like a drifter.

There are
many paths,
you can follow
in footsteps,
but you'll never
leave an impression
on the world.

The Unloved

I see the people.
Those that feel
unloved.

They search
dead ends,
and feel as though
they are missing.

Missing a piece
of something.

They feel lost,
wandering
through the darkness.
scared,

Living in fear
fear that their fire
might burn out.

Do not fear
the darkness
I see the fire
in your eyes.

Silence

She sits in
silence.

Silence
that hides,
a thousand
screams.

Behind a
broken smile,
and shattered
eyes.

Staring at
a world,

that can
only see
its own
reflection.

Heavy Soul

Life will take a toll,
on the strongest people.

The journey will add
burden,
with little things,
buried
under a thought.
deep,
deep,
down.
These things
will weigh on the soul,
until you stumble upon them.

In those moments,
when you dig
through
your thoughts
at night.

Your soul may weep,
just shovel them
into a pile,
and burn them.

In this moment,
you will learn
to let go,

as the smoke
uplifts
your
heavy soul.

Things will change.

Time will pass,

But it will not pass you by.

Every moment,

Belongs to you,

Because you are alive.

Half A Lifetime

I recognize your eyes.
It all came back to me.
The universe had let a secret slip,
and the next thing I knew it was gone.
But, for a moment
I knew,

I've always been with you.
It just took me
half a lifetime,
to physically
find you,

and as the memory
of that moment fades back
to the sky, hidden
in the stars.
I know I will love you
in this life,
and in the next one
I will find you.

Fragile

It's reckless and beautiful,
and love often is careless.
Don't let it
make your heart heavy.

Only the reckless
can love like you,
and only the beautiful
have such strength.

But the way you carry
your fragile heart
on your sleeve,

I just know,
such fragile things often break.

Dodge The Rain

We always chased it.
Still, she would calm
my storm.

And somehow,
she always
caught the sun,

even when
it would hide away.

We would sit,
and watch
for raindrops,

and somehow
dodge the rain.

Scars Of Diamond

You may feel fragile,
and fear being broken.
But you are strong
as diamond.

You will not break.
You cannot crack.
But you can be cut
a fragile diamond
like you is rare.
So they will try.

Don't worry about them,

the deeper the cut
the better the clarity,
and in the end
you'll wear scars,

made of diamond.

Bloom Into Eternity

I know you're there
in each gust of wind,
each beam of light.
and I will remember
that smile.

The way I remember that day
the medic moving in slow motion
as I watched your body wilt,

and saw your spirit walk free
to bloom into eternity.

Spectrum

He was a kind, quiet, young boy, wiser than his years;
so he chose to offer the world some silence.
A fitting gift in a place deafened by the cacophony of screams
vying for attention.

He would retreat to the corners of his mind.
A world of its own, where make believe and fantasy drown out
the cacophony;
where magic engulfs the silence.

Ironically, this silence drew the attention of men who shrink
minds. They poked and prodded their way around his world.
Disturbing the silence where the magic resides.
Those mind shrinking men diagnose, and decide, that a
spectrum of some kind reflects in his mind.

What they could not see is the magic, the light; ribbons
reflecting all the colours entwined.

Forgive them my boy for being colour blind.
They just cannot see your beautiful mind.

The Karmapa

Be humble,
and have faith.
That's what
the teacher said,

not with his mouth
or with his words
with something else instead,

was it what they call an aura?
That spoke
without a sound,
be humble,
and have faith.

So simple,
yet profound.
Humility is rare, I know,
and your faith may be covered in dust,

be humble,
and have faith my friend.
That is all I ask for us.

Listen
See

and understand
but never lose your way.

Place your feet
in another's shoes,
and don't be led astray.

Enlightenment
is a path within,
you are walking
it each day.

Be humble,
and have faith.
That's what
I heard him say.

Starfire

She shines
like a star.

She isn't dead inside,
waiting to burn out.

She is an ember,
that could set the world
ablaze,
and engulf it in
her flame.

Starfire
still gentle,
enough to warm your bones,

leaving embers as she walks away.

I'd watch them burn

as I try to feed her flame.

If only to keep her
a moment more.

Thunder Beings

On Narragansett sands,
the warm Niantic sun retreats.
As a cool Wampanoag breeze drifts in from the east.
The days get hot under the Niantic sun,
so with cedar wood and calloused hands,
I work well into the evening.
Taking a moment to look to the ocean,
to acknowledge the Wampanoag breeze,
and blow some smoke skyward,
like those who named this land.

Today though, the Nenemehkia come.
The Thunder-Beings.
The birds of thunder will roll in,
as they often do with summer storms.

This time of year it could seem to some,
that even the sky will go to war with itself.
The Niantic sun retreats into the thunder clouds.
The lightning comes quick with the smell of rain.
Then, the Nenemehkia disappear.
I look to the sky.
I want to roll with the Thunder-Beings.

Love Too Hard

Those that love too hard,
and those who throw stones
with the things they say.

Words that leave
their reckless lips,
Leave you shattered,
like broken glass.

As your bleeding finger tips
hold the pieces
in a heart shaped pane,

somehow
they always fix it,
and seal it with a kiss.

Moves The Sun & Stars

We will be
despite the miles,
or the oceans between us
we will be.

We are surrounded
by the kind of love
that moves the sun and stars.

A ferocious love
that cannot be tamed or broken,
A love that will fight back.

Some say certain things
 are meant to be.

We'll be a testament to that.

See Forever

Some memories
are kept forever
never forgotten,
and those we never made
to forget, somehow haunt us.

Stay with me tonight,
and as the moonlight
reflects in your eyes

let this be a moment
you'll see forever.

Guide You

You deserve it.
Love.

A love
that will fill
your darkest corner,
and chase down
sunlight through the storm.

A love
that will set
the moon alight,
and always
guide you
home.

Chance To Feel

The world stood still.

You move slowly,
passing smiling faces.
sick at the sight.

To smile whilst
the world stands still
is insane.

Soon you will notice,
it hasn't.

If it had
we would all
freefall together,
which would be
a romantic notion,
but it hasn't.

and all you can
do is feel
So just feel.

Some say it means
you are alive.

Really it means
you have a chance,

and as long as
you have that

You will never stand
still.

Horizon

I go to the same place
where the ocean
meets the sky,
and in this moment
I understand,
It is all an illusion.
The ocean will never
reach the sky.
As it mirrors the sun,
in an effort to grasp her light.
To cover the dark forgotten world
that swallows whole civilizations.
Unable to swim in its depths,

Now, I understand
you were my sky,
and I was your ocean.
Gripping your light
only for it to drown
in the depths of my soul.

As I reach out blindly,
and crash into the illusion.

You hold your breath,
and I somehow reach the sky.

Dawn

She would rise before the sun.
As I treat the minutes like hours,
somehow dreaming in thirty second intervals.

Never the same dream,
which always annoyed me,
like going to the movies
only to have the screen
burn out halfway through.

That has happened to me before.
They offer a refund.
It is not the same.

Dreams don't offer any compensation for interruption.

It was dawn.
A time that should be reserved for the birds,
as only they have the grace of early mornings.

As I turn the corner,
the sun and I would meet,
with a quick reminder,
that there are gods at work.

Blackbird

I sat down
to rest on warm grass;
a hot day
in late spring.

A day where the breeze
complements the sun,
working together in unison.

As the old oak tree
greets the sky
with a gentle wave.

I watch a blackbird
rest on a powerline,
next to the old brick chimney,
I should probably inspect for leaks.

Somehow, nature will always
find a way in,
no matter how skilled the labour.
She has time on her side,
and skills no man can master.

I watch the blackbird
make himself at home.

As if those lines
had been put there just for him.

I wonder if he understands
the power beneath him,
how it lights the darkness,
helps shelter souls
and warm cold bones.

I wonder if I'm a blackbird.

True Strength

Started early this year,
not as early as last year.
The gods have a sense of humour,
and covered us in a late frost last spring.
Seeds don't do well in the cold,
still, the cilantro and radishes made it.
They know something we don't,
and stay quiet.
A sign of true strength.

Paint The Sky

We will just sit,
as the sun & sky
begin to paint
tell me of your journey.
I will try to help
you along the way
as you look at me
and smile
uncertain what to say.
We will paint the sky with
diamond dust
to prove we made it there
one day.

Phoenix

She came in
and told me
everything.
Told me what
had happened.
Her heart
was on fire,
and this time,
I couldn't control
it.

All I could do
was hold her,
to stop her from
crumbling to ash.

Sometimes
that is all you can
do,
just hold someone,
to keep them
from falling
apart.

Then, something
strange happened,

and in that
moment
I saw her,
for the first time.

A phoenix in
the glint of her eye,
rising from the ashes
you left,
and in that moment
I realized
what I always
knew.

She was
a legend,
a myth,

a fantasy
you did not believe in.
You could not see her
for herself.

Wolves Know Better

They warn you
of the wolf.
The one who
will tell you
you are lost,
in an effort to
herd you.

To give the best
of you away
with broken
attempts
to tell you
what to do
what to think
and what to feel.

These are the
fools
in sheep's clothing.

The wolves know better.

Dog Jokes

They say dogs laugh.
That deep, heavy pant
that happy proud dogs do.

The old boy is laughing
next to me now.
Don't know what's funny.
Must be an inside joke
with the crows.

He never used to laugh
never wagged his tail,
or sniffed the sky.
Most people he met still
own a scar to remember him by.
Mine is on my left hand.

Trying to get something out of a dog that
doesn't trust, never ends well. Most won't
come within three feet of him now, which I
think he prefers.

I find that spot behind his ear.
Funny how things change, I thought.
The old boy laughed,
and let me in on the joke.

Stockholm Syndrome

You took me hostage
with a smile.
came in and
killed them all
with barely a stare.

We've been on the run,
and after all this time
you are still a reminder
of something no one will find.

Distant music
a melody playing in our
getaway car.

As we drive
for hours on end,
and always know
where we are.

Dreamcatcher

Tonight
let her sleep,
and as the darkness
creeps in
catch her
dreams.

Keep her
company
under the
moonlight.

Hands Of Time

Those
Tired hands
Holding
Time
Must be losing
Their grip.

Can't tell
If it's noon or night
On a day like this.

Time

Time is a nuisance.

The universe holds time in contempt.
Turning hours into decades

distant planets,
trillions of galaxies.

Here, it is six pm.

An ocean away,
eleven pm.

The universe keeps watch
with starry eyes
as we try
to add the hands
of a clock.
days weren't
good enough for us.

Like everything we must dissect.
Man and his machine mind,

Don't let a clock
steal your days.

Today

Remember
all things that pass,
and cherish all that is.

Eventually, it too will pass,
buried in the history books.
Forgotten under poetry, music,
myth and legend,

paying little attention to the present,
as the future is just too pressing,

the old days
are always
the good days,

and for some
reason
we never think
today
could be
one of
them

until it is.

Seize The Night

Held the night gently

The moonlight
was made for us,
made for madmen and lovers.

To seize the night,
and leave the day
for the sound of mind.

We would reach
the edge of galaxies,
as we chased down
shooting stars.

They always slip
through your fingertips.
But you can catch them
with your eyes.

Memories Remain

As time carves
destiny into the stars,
like a river
through a canyon,
or a lover's name
etched on your heart.

We are all waiting
for something.

Something
that might burn
slowly
Into a memory.

Gently placed
on a loved one's mantle.

Drink The Rain

We live without notice.
Memories remind us
to stay
in the moment.
But they often retreat
to the back of the mind
until it's too late.
When most run through life
the lucky ones wander slowly, through the
clouds,
Drinking the rain, as they walk with
thunder.
They know the path down here is
crowded.
People running,
in all directions.
Some into walls,
too busy keeping their head down.
Walk in the clouds
wander slowly,
and if you're lucky you will quench your
thirst,
and walk with the thunder,
and when you get there, look for me.
We'll trade a few good stories around the
fire.

Define You

Experience defeat
Face rejection.

These moments
will not define us.
We can wallow in them
for a while if we must.

Just remember this;
the world is littered
with people who will
try to break you
in an attempt to
fix themselves.

They do not
define you.

Chasing Shadows

As you search
you may run
into dead ends.

Chasing shadows,
and although there is
a long way to go
just know
I, too, feel lost;
we all do.

No one has quite figured it out.
There is something out there,
and you will find it.

Probably when you are so lost
you couldn't possibly be found.

Mermaid

I found her
by the ocean.
She had a way
about her
The way she
would handle things.

I watched her hold
honesty and love
above the waves.

They tried to
drown her,
and she could
always breathe,

Part of her
always
belonged to
the sea.

Poet With A Blind Eye

Fog rolls in
with thunder,

as the blackbirds
watch from
the treetops.

The music of the
gods,
said the poet
with a blind eye.

On days like this
you can hear
the clouds
as they serenade
the sky,

Ricochet

I sit in a dark room
at night
I watch the stars.

My mind tends to
drift away up there
kicking up stardust.

It reached the heavens
once,
It found the meaning
of life.

I heard it plummet
back
down,
and ricochet
against my skull.

I seem to have
lost what it found.

Fight For Her

Pay attention
when she gives you
that look.

The one that will
let you
in for a moment
a split second
too many miss.

You will see her
fighting
fighting back
every damn thing
she hides
so well,
and if she
lets you in,

fight for her,
and know
you have found
a place
you will never want
to leave.

Cursed By Hindsight

She could
always see
straight
through them.

Somehow blessed
with perfect sight,
the rest of us
cursed
to wait and see.

The mind
makes us many ages
hands of time can heal
or firmly take hold.

Fireflies

I don't weep
for lovers.
They tend to break
their own hearts.

I found that place
to weep for others.

As two fireflies
flickered by,

they disappeared
into the stars.

Stale Words

Damn poets
have made words stale.
The sentiment
has been choked
out of every
I love you.

As they grip at stones,
in search of water.

So forgive me,
I will not tell you I love you
I will not tell you I need you
I will not tell you
that I see
your face echo
in moon soaked streams.

I will not tell you
how the smell of salt air
fills every corner
of my mind with your
laughter,

or that I can stare
straight through the sun

after looking in your eyes.
Lost in a galaxy
mankind will never
be able to explore.

I will not tell you
that I hear your name
in every bird's song,
and each rumble of thunder.

How the sky fills with rain
as you leave,
and how the peonies open when
you return.

I will not tell you
I love you
I will not stale these words.

Children Of Earth

Wild
children of earth
bending the rules
as we go.

Send men up in fire
to a tin can, that floats
further than the sky.
Just out of reach of time.

Takes four hours to get back
through the atmosphere,
falling from the sky.

Takes eight to fly
across the Atlantic,
falling comes naturally to us.

Mother earth owns the rule book
ensuring these men can't walk for a day,
as they feel gravity
as if It is the first time.
Must be humbling
to feel the hand of God
gripping you firmly
to the ground.

Sparrow

I watch
a sparrow
kick up dust
then dart into
the light.
disappearing
into the heavens
for a moment.

She had told me of
a courtyard
in medieval England
full of sparrows.

I'd watch her
as she fanned
her wings,
and the sun
would slip through
their feathered tips.

She would dream
of the clouds,
and everything
they hide from our eyes.

Dodge The Rain

Her mind would soar
as she would
look to the sky.

I think
she was a sparrow
in another life,

Seeds Of Stardust

Eventually
we all have to go,
and if you must go
leave it all.

Every piece,
scattered
like wildflowers

strewn
across the stars
of every soul
you've touched.

As you take root
in places
you could never
set foot.

You will remain.

Eternal.

Maybe .
we could live
a little more
harmoniously
if we remember
who we are.

The Wild One

She ran wild
into that
lonely
mountain
stream.

Ripples
from her
heartbeat
put the stars
just out of reach.

As she tried
to pluck them
from the
water's surface.

Mind Of A Giant

Where do we go
from here?
I've been walking
for a while now
not sure where,
but no one is.
So we will keep
going.

We lack the mind
of a giant.
We don't have
the memory,
or the sense of self,
and we seem to
have forgotten
where we are
headed.

Opinions Of The Lost

You question yourself.
You know
the answers are there.
Somewhere,
buried
beneath
all the opinions
of the lost.

Lost
in search of something,
anything with the grit
to rid away the dust
under our skin.

To restore our faith
in us

A simple reminder
of who we are.

Something More

I thought
for a moment
what the miles had done.

Many travelers better than I
lay buried under their dreams.
Under the pillar
of who they thought
we could be.

We have come too far
to turn back.
Tearing at each other,
we have clawed
too deep inside
of it all.

Learned a little
too much
for our own good.
Empty hearts and a mind
dull of fear.
We have become a
manifestation of all we see
and forgotten to feel
for something more.

With A Smile

And some give
themselves away

with a smile.

Others take
what they can get.

The truth is

we never know
how much.

We give and take

until it's gone.

Lighthouse

She stood strong
against the rain.
All the storms
in my soul could not wash her away.

My lighthouse
that kept me afloat
when everything else
began to sink.

And sometimes, you have to sink,
to weather the storm on your own,
and all we ever really need
is a guiding light.

Whiskey & Amaretto

Like love

It numbs your lips,
and always goes down
with a fierce, gentle burn.

It's that sweet aftertaste
that gets you drunk,
and coming back for more.

Lost & Found

She would look
for herself
in others.

In all the things
that might make her
remember,
she swore to the sky
she was looking for love.

Really, just trying
to feel.

Tried to understand
what it was
they said,
as her demons
speak in tongues.

She found herself
In memories
not in anyone.

Setting Sun

I would lose myself
in her beauty.

She was the sky.

But it was the rain,
and the ocean tides
beneath her skin.

that made me fall into her,
and drown for a chance

to hold her last setting sun.

Ride Mountains

I look for
The dreamers
The lonely
The broken
The few

The ones who ride mountains.

The wild ones
who pierce the night,
with eyes of fire,
and set the skies ablaze.

Wild

Run wild.
They envy the untamed,
and will attempt
to break your spirit.
Run wild,

and when they come
to tame the world

leave me here
for a little while.

So I might find
what is still wild.

Patchwork Quilt

Maybe somewhere
along the way, I'll read
your mind someday.

In a book that sits on bookshop shelves
with Shakespeare and Hemingway.

One that sends an inspired spark with the
turn of every page,
with tales that sit in memory no matter the
reader's age.

Imagine if all of this,
came to you one day,
the world lends its ear would you speak
clear?
Or not utter a single phrase?

What of your opinions,
that you keep hidden away,
underneath your patchwork quilt
of what you're supposed to say.

Foggy Night

In people I see myself
I hear the voices
I see the faces.
I've left pieces of me
I've taken pieces of them,

We all do,
without notice,
some help us see
through the fog,
and we find beauty.

Others we must bury
deep down.

On a foggy night like this

I feel like I'm looking
through another set of eyes,
and I start to wonder
where I've left mine.

The Angels

She had been through hell,
and captured its fire
with the same eyes
that read
omens,
and signs.

She knew
The gods speak in birds,
and how time meant more than
numbers, and clock hands.

It was the way
she spoke
with the Angels.

Rebuilt

You rebuilt yourself.
When life ran up
from behind and
left you.

In a million pieces
when they all just stood
around and watched.

You picked through
broken pride.
You pieced together
shattered dreams.

You rebuilt yourself.

Matches

Joy without sorrow
is no longer joy,
and love without pain
is simply emptiness.

This is our curse,
it is our blessing.

It's the numb ones
who will watch
their world burn,

with the matches
in their hand.

Miracle

And in the end
if it all just
fades to black

just know
this was
our miracle,
and nothing
can
take that.

Star Dreamers

There are
dreamers out there

who will find
other worlds,
and etch
their name
into the stars.

Today they found one
with two suns.

A lightyear from us
they say.
that's only trillions of miles away.

St. Francis

Met St. Francis
somewhere in Assisi.

Sat surrounded
with God's creatures.

Not in a cathedral,
where flickering flames
carry a prayer.

I still lit a candle,
to keep her
spirit burning.

Mother Nature

She held fire and water.
She was made of the earth,

and when she spoke
the sky would thunder.

and when she wept
raindrops fell
from her hair.

Her tears could
flood,
as her eyes held hurricanes,

with the storms
to cleanse her soul.

The heavens rested
in those eyes,
and as she slept
day turned to night.

Fight

We fought
to get here.
Remember this.

We fought
everyone,
and everything.

And we wouldn't
change that,

or we would
have lost
ourselves
in the fight.

Our Scars

We knew
the safe path.
We must have
enjoyed
the hard road.

We wore
our scars
well,
and let
the world know.

We were willing
to live
for a moment.

Soulless

You see them
in streets and avenues.

Some lose it
along the way.
Some sell it
to the devil in disguise,
and although you
could never
be one of them.

You will meet many,
and the demons within them
will attempt to fill their void
with all that is within you.

Hold on to your soul.

Leave It With Me

Leave yourself with me.

I will keep you
with all the things I guard.

With all the secrets
that would scar their souls.

I will keep you.
wherever you go.

When you cannot find
yourself.

Find me
in those moments
you feel lost.
When you are stood
in the cold.
Broken and scattered.

Find me in these moments,
and I will make you whole.

We must have had

lion hearts.

We left

scorched earth,

and would watch

our bridges burn

in flames for our

pride.

Something Rotten

Behind the veil
there is something
rotten.

Every now and then
the wind blows wild enough
for us to catch a glimpse.

We all know it's not just
our eyes playing tricks on us,

and I hear the wind howling.

Thoughts

Don't give
too many thoughts
to the darkness.

Save some
for the light.

They say thoughts
make us
who we are,
and that will always
sound
like a threat.

Constellations

I did not bring us here
you did.
Carrying everything you love,
and everything you hate.

Creasing everything
you hold too tight.
While you gently grasp
what you
could never touch.

Now, I ask you
to let go,
and hold me tight.

As gently
as those who could
never feel you,
the way I do.

When I'm beneath your stars
counting the constellations.

Mason

She built walls
around
her broken heart.
Sealed
with empty
expectations.

No doors,
no windows,

Just cold stone walls,

I rubbed my knuckles raw
To be a master mason,

and cut through the stone.

Gallery

I want to be inside
you.
Inside your
mind,

In the dark
corners with
all of your
cobwebs.

I want to see
all the hidden
pieces,
Beautifully lost in
your gallery,
in a puzzle
I will never try to solve,
for the possibility to stay.

Completely covered
in your canvas.

With every brushstroke
they never took the time
to see.

Hearts Of Gold

There is a fire
in you and I.
We were born
with it.

Everything that is born
has this fire.

But it doesn't burn like ours.
Wild and uncontrolled.

We had to learn to sift
through ash
for traces of gold,
and we coated our
hearts in it.

Now covered
with the tooth marks
of those who questioned us,
and now they know.
We cannot be broken.

We are all too real.

All too rare.

Attachments

I had to learn to never
get too attached to one place.

That isn't easy when you feel
so attached to everything.

We're never the same person
who returns.

Sometimes, I feel it tear away,
and leave a wound
that will inevitably turn to a scar.
Most of the time
they cling like a feather,
and fall just as faint.

Attach me
to your secrets,
all the things
you could never give away,
and I will always keep them
company.

Strangers

You looked
too deep,
skipping
between
your head
and your
heartbeat.

We had become
stranded.

Left in a moment
that will tumble
endlessly
through time.

Found in
a lonely thought
then gone.

Without ever
exchanging
a word.

Roulette
& Six-Shooters

I told you why I don't gamble
I've seen more than fingers
get broken.
But you took the bet.
Now you're stuck
with someone
who hates to lose,
and loves to play
roulette.
As long as they load
the six-shooter.

Whiskey Eyes

Vintage
I could tell
by the color
of the eyes
made to age
with grace.

The kind
you drink straight.

Can never
put her down,

before
the ice
melts away.

Paris In September

Her eyes emulate the light
of Paris in September.

Staring darkness
in the face,
she didn't flinch.

At night those eyes
hold the light
of a thousand stars.

As darkness
succumbs to her stare,
She will always see

what is
before it turns
to what was.

Immortal Love

If love is war
then
fight for it.

He had his head
in the sand.
Survived,
to let love die
a thousand times.

We'll run our
frontline.
in every firefight,
with an immortal love.

Sunstone

I do not know
where you went.

You said you found a sunstone,
and each reflection of light
led you to another world.

Through the darkness,
through the clouds,

and of all the things
you have found,

I hope you find
all you are looking for.

Implode

I am my savior,
and my worst enemy.

I will hold the light with the dark,
and they will never touch.

Yet, like the edges of the earth
they are always connected,

and you kept me spinning.
to stop it all imploding
into weightless dust.

Closer To God

"The closest thing to God"
she said.

Trimming the roses,

The kind that climb to the sun
in an effort to lose themselves,
and detach from a world of thorns.

She helped them along the way.

K.C. Kemp

Cost Of Landing

We reached the edge,
and it was time to
take a leap
of faith.

Words have their way.

A glimpse
into the future.

A bird taking flight
that will never
pay the cost
of landing.

Reaching
everything.

Everything that is,
and all that could be.

If only we take off
on time
under her patient wing.
To glide forever,
disappearing

when need be,

Knowing nothing
ever ends.

It all goes on
with, or
without us,
and that
is what makes
a moment,

worth living.

Four thirty
again
These nights,
waiting for
sleep to set in.
and I feel you
next to me.
Lost in the most
vivid dreams
waiting for the
moon to set.

Passion

We do not understand it.
All this passion
this burning passion
that leaves its mark
within us all.

It is too violent
to ignore.
searing
through bones.
Spouting roses from our skulls.

a reminder
you are not alone,
not the only one
that glows red-hot
for something more.

For someone
to make us more,
and I, too,
need someone.

Someone like you
to tend to the fire.

Stood With You

I do not want to cause trouble.
I want you to know
you are loved,
and there is beauty,
and good
still in this world.
I want to ignite,
within you
within the
deepest parts of you,
Everything that you believe
defines you.

I want you to know you are more.
I want you to know that if you stand,
others will find the strength,
and I want you to know that when you
stand,
I'll be stood with you.

Wise Soul

I met a wise soul once.
We'll meet many
throughout our lives.
Sometimes, we'll get lucky,
and they stick around for the ride.

Some teach
and remind us
why we have come.
An old dog.
taught me more about life and it's spirit
than any school or religion ever could.
He taught patience,
and that life has teeth,
and to approach it with respect and trust.
It is not to be coddled, or neglected.
It is to love, and believe that there is
something unspoken that binds us.

Life will show its teeth,
Sometimes, it will bite,
and sometimes,
it'll give you a gentle nudge,
curl up at your feet,
and keep watch while you sleep.

Armor

Forgive me,
I do not tread lightly.
I will not make a sound.

I will leave a mark
in places you
never knew were there.

Until you lay down your armor,
and find my name carved into
your heart.

Aware

I know what it is like
to lay awake
aware of everything.

Aware of your thoughts
as words replay
in your head.
Moments you have captured,
and your head
is trying to understand
what your heart cannot.

You got a good heart kid
it is just too big,
too big for its own good.

That is why
the world needs you.

Keep beating
you will understand soon.

Secrets

Words complicate everything,
and the eyes often only tell you
what you want to know.

True secrets are like that
you have to really
know a person to see
their secrets.
to know what they hide,
what they bury.

Often so deep
they cannot find it them self.

You have to have mapped
more than the stars within them.
even a gut feeling that
slowly sinks into a bitter truth
can be misleading.

We often break
our own hearts
with our
own minds,
and that is
our own madness.

With You

It's funny how
we lay here.
Minutes
stretch
into hours,
into years
with you
it felt
like time stood still.

Things change,
people come,
people go.

Yet, you are still here,
and time will always stop
when I am here with you.

When I stare too long at the sky,
I start to see the rain.
It is rain I cannot feel.
It is this rain that feels familiar,
and the sky will always remember,
Those the world forgot.

If I could hold you
If I could show you
If I could have you
One more day.

Gypsy blood
runs through
these veins
I must travel on,
always be the wanderer
the road will be home.

<u>Coming soon</u>
Wildflowers
Bloom
In the dark

Follow on instagram : k.c.kemp
Email: kckemp@outlook.com

www.ingramcontent.com/pod-product-compliance
Lightning Source LLC
Chambersburg PA
CBHW021155020426
42331CB00003B/64